Parables of Hope

PARABLES OF HOPE

By Alicia Snyder

Noemata Publishing 2013

Cover Photography by Richard Snyder
Used by Permission.

PARABLES OF HOPE
Alicia Snyder
Noemata Publishing
ISBN-13: 978-1493616442
ISBN-10: 1493616447

Printed by CreateSpace, an Amazon.com Company.

For Grace

Contents

HOW THIS BOOK CAME TO BE

The Lord Jesus Christ rescued me from the depths of despair and hopelessness. When I was helplessly trapped in selfishness and self-righteousness, He showed me that He had given His blood to redeem me. He had conquered death to free me from myself and make me His very own.

Soon after I learned to know His love in a personal way, God brought a tiny infant into my life. I opened my heart to Ricky out of newfound love for my Savior, who says that welcoming one little child is the same as welcoming Him.[1] Watching Ricky's trusting ways taught me much about my relationship with my heavenly Father.

A few years later, God allowed me to establish a friendship with Grace Smith. Her faithfulness paved the way for me to learn lessons of hope and trust and to express these ideas in words. Without her, the words and drawings in this book would never have existed.

Through all of life, my father offered his faithful prayers and encouragement. The grace of God expressed through my father's prayers form the basis for each of the blessings in my life. His encouragement led me to compile and publish the lessons God has taught me.

As I began work on this book, God provided lavishly through a number of generous people. Helen Roseveare, a respected missionary doctor to the Congo, graciously allowed me to use the story of the acacia tree arrows, a story which had deeply impacted my life. Richard Snyder, a photographer and missionary to Nigeria, donated the use of his beautiful photography for the cover. Amy Bloyer gave her time to provide helpful editorial suggestions. Christina, Paul, Anne, Lois, and Siegfried Snyder spent hours editing the manuscript and giving input on formatting and design.

Finally, Ricardo Berumen and his mother generously gave permission to share his stories. Three years after most of the incidents in the book took place, his trustful and joyful attitude continue to bring me great joy.

Skippy

One

SKIPPY'S REDEMPTION

Tears trickled slowly down my face as I gazed into the silent starry night. One by one, the luscious tidbits of turkey scraps fell unheeded onto the compost pile. I could hardly stand the emptiness.

For thirteen years, our little black Schipperke dog had waited for me on Thanksgiving night, her bright eyes sparkling out of her midnight black fur. When I approached each year with Thanksgiving leftovers, Molly's joy was almost uncontainable. Wagging her whole body in anticipation, she licked my hand repeatedly. Her gratefulness made giving to her a delight.

My little black Molly had been a great friend and pet. Not only did she revel in my gifts, but she had a zest for living and for the fact that she was mine. Although she had her short-comings, she showered me with sincere expressions of delight in me and all I gave her. She often wrapped her paws around me affectionately, looked into my face compassionately, or simply raced around the yard in circles of sheer, unconstrained delight.

After thirteen joyful years of life, Molly had used her last ounces of strength to nibble a treat I brought to her one October day. Her eyes looked wearily up at me in one last expression of gratefulness. That afternoon, she died.

A few months after that lonely Thanksgiving Day, we bought a full-grown dog named Skippy. Our new dog was a small black Schipperke just like Molly, with many of the same familiar mannerisms that I missed so much. I hoped Skippy would help to fill the void that Molly had left. Most of all, I looked forward to giving her treats and seeing her delight.

But the first morning after we brought Skippy home, my anticipation turned to dismay. As I stood in front of her, opening a can of special treats, Skippy didn't lick me gratefully. Instead, she hurtled her tiny body into the air and wildly snatched the treat right out of my hand. Although her ability to jump astounded me, her response was shocking and bewildering. I hoped that when Skippy had adjusted to our home and learned our rules, everything would be better.

But in the days to come, Skippy's sense of entitlement only deepened. When I gave her my undivided attention, Skippy was calm. But if I even walked by without petting her, Skippy would transform into a snarling, angry beast. No matter how much time I spent with her, she always demanded more.

Although we tried to train Skippy and give her guidelines, she became more and more self-centered and fierce. Before long, I dreaded going near my dog.

When Skippy was upset, everyone knew about it. She would angrily bite someone, haughtily chew something, or pull down laundry that was drying in the sun. Dragging the clean clothes under a nearby bush, she piled them in the dirt and sat on top of them as if to say, "I deserve much more than you give me."

One Sunday, I went outside after church to spend some time petting Skippy. I loved having a dog and getting to enjoy her company on long Sunday afternoons. But before I even reached down to pet her, Skippy jumped up, ripping my best blouse with her small, sharp teeth. I immediately forgot my desire to pet her. Skippy's selfishness was making it impossible for her to see the love I intended for her.

One day, Skippy's life came to a standstill. As four-year-old Ricky played with his punch ball, Skippy alternated between frenzied excitement and feverish snarling. Tired of playing with Skippy, Ricky threw the ball over the fence that bordered the backyard. As he opened the gate to retrieve it, Skippy darted out. Quickly the dog disappeared from sight. We had no idea which direction she had gone.

After a long and fruitless search for Skippy, Ricky and I returned home to the news that the vet had called. Skippy had darted across a busy street and was instantly hit by a car. Before we had any idea what had happened, another driver had rescued her and taken her to the vet. To save her life, it would cost us six times the amount we had purchased her for in the first place.

"Should we really pay to save this dog?" we wondered. She was dangerous and destructive, and didn't deserve to be rescued from her own bad choices.

Conflicting voices and opinions kept circulating in our minds and hearts.

"Skippy is a liability. We have considered putting her to sleep for weeks. Now is a perfect opportunity."

"There is no way to justify spending that much money to save a dog like Skippy. For Molly, it might have been worth it to pay so much, but not for a dog like this."

"Yes, but somehow I can't escape the thought that life has value."

Although it didn't make sense, we finally decided to pay for the operation that would save our dog's life.

Skippy came home a few days later with three legs and an ear-splitting smile that lingered even when the treats were gone and her caregivers had other chores to do.

When her incision healed, she learned to sit politely and wait for her breakfast to be served. She tried not to bark at dogs she met on her daily outings. Even though she regained her ability to walk, run, and jump, she never again pulled down laundry. Her life had changed completely.

We paid a high price to rescue our enemy, and she became our devoted friend.

What a beautiful picture of redemption! Each of us was created by God for a close relationship with Him. He longs to be generous to us even more than I longed to show my generosity to Skippy.[2] But we as humans refuse to thank Him, turning instead to greed, selfishness, hatred, dishonesty, and lust.[3] Our selfish sense of entitlement makes it impossible for us to recognize His lavish goodness and love.

Skippy was near death because she ran away from her loving masters. In the same way, we deserve eternal death when we disobey and run from God. Jesus Christ chose to take the punishment our sin deserves. To do this, He paid the highest price possible to rescue us from death. That price was His own blood, His own sinless life.

By dying on the cross, Jesus generously paid the price to save us, His enemies. Three days later, He came alive again to invite us to become His friends. When we understand His undeserved kindness, we come to Him with hearts of faith, trusting His love and power.[4] Like Skippy, we are not saved because we are good or smart or loving.[5] But after we understand and accept the price Jesus paid for our salvation, His Spirit helps us change our actions and attitudes because of our love for Him. We want to serve and obey our Savior because we realize He is our most loyal companion and our truest friend.[6]

For while we were still helpless, at the appointed time, Christ died for the ungodly. For rarely will someone die for a just person—though for a good person perhaps someone might even dare to die. But God proves His own love for us in that while we were still sinners, Christ died for us. Much more then, since we have now been declared righteous by His blood, we will be saved through Him from wrath.

Romans 5:6-9

Two

SKITTISH

Gordon Dunlap stepped closer to Monet, speaking softly to the horse. Monet raised her head nervously, then darted away. Gordon turned toward his audience and explained what he was about to do.[7]

Monet was a yearling Arabian horse who had recently become fearful and difficult to approach. Perhaps she had been chased by a neighbor dog that persistently jumped the fence and barked at her. Or perhaps a wind storm had blown plastic sacks and debris around her corral, inducing panic. Without an experienced master who knew how to teach her which things were valid causes for fear and which things were harmless, Monet now subscribed to the principle, "Run first, ask questions later."[8]

Today, Gordon approaches quietly with the offer of experienced and gentle leadership. As she sees him coming, Monet panics. Darting back and forth, she nervously tries to get past Gordon into the freedom of the open field.

"She thinks the answer is somewhere out there," Gordon explains, motioning toward the open corral. "I want her to learn that the answer is in me. I am the one who is going to be controlling her emotions, and I am the one who is going to be giving her rest."[9]

Learning to trust will be a long process, but Gordon knows that the first step is gaining eye contact. In order to earn the horse's trust he must first earn her gaze. If she refuses to look at him, she will never see the kindness written all over his face.

With encouraging words and soothing tones, Gordon walks toward her again and again. As she backs away, he guides her into a corner. He will not let her out until she finally makes eye contact.

"I'm keeping her in this corner," he explains. "I want those two eyes."

Finally, the horse looks up at him. She has no other choice. She is desperate. The kindness she sees both startles and confuses her.

When their eyes meet, Gordon immediately backs off. He wants to give Monet some space to make her own decision. Will she come to him of her own free will?

Gordon continues this process for several days. Each time he trains her, Gordon comes as close as he can. He speaks to her gently and showers her with encouragement. He moves to the right when he wants her to run to the right. When he turns, she turns. He wants her to understand that even in her fear, he is in control of where she goes and what she does.

After several sessions, Monet begins to make eye contact more frequently. Seeing his love and capability, trust grows in her heart. Sometimes she lets fear win the day, running away as he approaches. But most of the time, she allows him to come near and stroke her reassuringly.

Finally the day comes when Gordon introduces the halter. Gently and confidently, he allows her to sniff it. A halter will no longer mean torment and confinement, he assures her. She will be much happier when she is under the control of a loving and trustworthy master.

"Good girl!" Gordon croons. "This is comfort. That's all it is. It's just comfort."

In Psalm 32, God offers the powerful illustration of horsemanship. David had experienced a time of deep pain, hurt, and sin. God reassured David that His forgiveness reached to the depth of the heart to heal and restore. Not only would God heal him, but He would direct him tenderly, like a trustworthy master. David did not need to fear the steps that he took toward God.

But David would have to come to God of his own free will. God wanted David to place his gaze on the Lord and freely submit to His leadership. God did not want a follower who was like a horse, unwilling to come unless caught and bridled.

There are times when God's gentle hand, His loving offers, and His plans for our lives seem like confinement and torment. We pray for His guidance, but shy away when He comes near. When cornered, looking to Him brings hope. Accepting His offer of guidance and direction brings security. And slowly, sometimes painfully, it brings the realization that His will is not torment or confinement or imprisonment. It is comfort. Just comfort.

"I will instruct you and show you the way to go; with My eye on you, I will give counsel.

"Do not be like a horse or mule, without understanding, that must be controlled with bit and bridle or else it will not come near you."

Psalm 32:8-9

Three

NEVER ALONE

"You're leaving me." A little face looked up into mine. His gaze was imploring, fearful, and sincere. "Don't leave me."

I had been invited to help sponsor a youth sleepover at my church. I had agreed to go, figuring that the boy I babysat would be picked up before it was time to leave. If not, I would leave him with my parents for a few minutes.

But his mom had not come yet and it was almost time for me to leave. Ricky's brown eyes were gazing into mine, begging me to stay with him.

Quickly gathering my pajamas, I tried to think of all I would need. Time was running out and I was not finished packing. As I packed, however, little Ricky was following me.

This little one was not a babysitting job. Far from being a job, he was a precious treasure and solemn responsibility. I had prayed for and watched over him since infancy with a passion that sprang from newfound love for my Savior and Creator.

Normally happy to stay with my family for a few minutes, today he was unusually distraught. Changes and separation in his home had upset his stability. And now his faithful babysitter was packing up and preparing to go.

"Don't go," he begged. "This is your home. You live here. Never leave this home."

Quietly, I realized what he was thinking. He thought I was moving out, something that had recently happened in his household.

I could afford to be a few minutes late to the sleepover in order to add some stability and reassurance to a little life. I would wait to leave until after his mom had picked him up.

Although I still needed to pack before I could leave, I calmly spoke: "I won't leave you."

I was pulling my sheets out of the closet when I became aware that a little face was looking into mine. His face was distorted with fear.

"Don't leave me. You're leaving me."

I had already promised him I wouldn't leave. Didn't he believe me?

"You're not talking to me. You're leaving me."

"I promised you, I will not leave you."

"But you're getting ready to go. You're leaving me."

As I finished packing, Ricky's tears and questions continued to come. As he crumpled wearily on the couch, I stroked his forehead and reassured him that I would not leave. Finally, he fell into a troubled sleep. He simply could not understand how I could promise one thing and yet seem to be doing another.

As I sat beside his sleeping form, I was pricked to the heart. How often do I respond to God in the same way? God speaks His promises quietly and simply through His word. But when I see circumstances pointing in another direction, I immediately doubt.

Moses had the same struggle when called to take the people out of Egypt. Despite the fact that God had promised to let His people go, things were only getting worse. He said, "Why did you ever send me? Ever since I went in to Pharaoh to speak in Your name he has caused trouble for this people, and You haven't delivered Your people at all."

"You shall see," God replied.[10]

Later, when Moses questioned God's power to bring meat to the people, God gave the same response: "Is the LORD's power limited? You will see whether or not what I have promised will happen to you."[11]

God's promise to be with His children is unchanged and unchangeable. Sometimes God seems silent and unresponsive. Circumstances seem to shout that He is no longer present.

But we have His word. No matter how much it looks like He has forsaken us, God promises,

"Do not fear, for I am with you; Do not anxiously look about you, for I am your God. I will strengthen you, surely I will help you, Surely I will uphold you with My righteous right hand."

Isaiah 41:10 NASB

Focused Hen

Four

FOCUSED

When a hen prepares to hatch baby chicks, she stops laying eggs. She gathers a group of eggs and fluffs up her feathers, getting ready to sit for three weeks straight. During those three weeks, she is focused. She can't get distracted by delicious food scraps or juicy worms. She has to stay on her eggs or they will die.

The hen is so focused that it's almost comical. You can put food right in front of her and she will stare at it like she's never seen food before. You can call her and she won't come. You can take her off her nest and set her on the ground and she'll just stay there in a little heap, wishing she were still on the nest.

God's word says that when we are doing something God wants us to do, we should be immovable like a mother hen. When God tells us to do something to show our love for Him, we shouldn't budge or get up or get distracted. God instructs believers to be "firmly sitting," "without moving," firmly persistent.[12] We should continue on in doing what God commands because our weary toil is not in vain.[13]

The hen persists despite the fact that her work is making no perceptible difference. Her eggs are as smooth and hard as they were the day she began sitting on them. A simple observer has no way to tell if the white spots of life on the yellow yolks have developed into thriving baby chicks or if the insides of the eggs are on their way to turning brown and putrid.

At the same time, the hen seems un-productive. She does nothing at all for days on end. Not only has she stopped laying eggs, but she has stopped contributing in any way to the life of the flock. She barely has time to eat, let alone participate with other hens.

The hen's job is a lonely job. Day and night, she spends her time in a dark corner, barely moving. No one sees what she is doing. No one commends her for turning the eggs from top to bottom in the morning and flipping them back in the evening.

If your service for Christ seems boring, lonely, useless, or repetitive, think again. Nothing can compare with the confident joy of a mother hen whose tender balls of fuzz have emerged and are cheeping contentedly from the safety of her warm feathers. One day, on earth or in heaven, your faithfulness will be rewarded. Until that day, let nothing move you.

Therefore, my beloved brethren,
be steadfast, immovable,
always abounding in the work of the Lord,
knowing that your toil is not in vain in the Lord.

1 Corinthians 15:58 NASB

Focused Friends

One hen sits all through the day.
Rooster crows and chickens play.

One hen sits all through the night.
Not another hen in sight.

Other hens are eating, squawking,
Clucking, scratching, pecking, walking.

Why does one hen never move?
Hen sits still to show her love.

Under feathers, eggs are warm
Under feathers, safe from harm.

Eggs will hatch if hen will stay,
Warm them in a faithful way.

One day, two days, three days, four.
Hen is lonely, wanting more.

Five days, six days, seven, eight.
How much longer can she wait?

Eggs are quiet, eggs are smooth…
Is this doing any good?

When will come day twenty-one?
This quiet job is not much fun.

Friend is coming, coming near.
"Are you lonely? Never fear."

Hen's friend tells her, "I will stay
Close beside you all the way.

"Together we will never move.
Together we will show our love.

"Eggs will hatch if we will stay,
Warm them in a faithful way.

"Soon will come day twenty-one.
With a friend it's much more fun.

"When our days to sit are past,
Our faithful friendship still will last."

Priceless Drawing

Five

PRICELESS

A few years ago, I drew a picture for my friend. This was no easy sketch. I wanted to make a beautiful drawing that looked as much like the original photograph as possible.

If you had been in my house during those weeks, you would have seen me bending over the picture, lost in thought. Sometimes I would draw diligently. Other times I would erase vigorously. Sometimes I would just spend minutes staring at the two pictures and trying to see the differences between them.

As I poured hours of time and effort into the picture, it quickly became priceless to me. I could have printed a picture off the computer that would have been more perfect than the drawing I made. It would have been more exact and more similar to the original. But my picture, with all its flaws, was valuable to me because I had spent so many loving hours working on it.

Further, the drawing was precious to me because of what it represented. Not only was I drawing a picture as a gift for a treasured friend, but I was also creating an image of a little boy I loved deeply. The combination stirred my heart to care intensely about the welfare of my picture.

Because it was so precious, I protected it carefully. I tucked it away in a manila folder, far from the grasp of little hands. On the rare occasion that I had to take it out and show it to someone, I held it carefully with a watchful eye. Especially when children were around, I was ceaselessly vigilant. I warned them not to even consider touching it. I would do almost anything to make sure that no one ruined my picture in any way.

I had begun the picture with uncertainty, but as I continued working, I became determined to finish it. I had already spent so much time on the picture, and I was very sure that I would finish what I had started.

During long hours of working, I considered the care with which God works on His children's lives. He could have chosen to instantly transform you and me into the image of His Son, but instead He chose a route that would take tireless effort and patient care.[14] He spends years and years erasing sin and mistakes, helping us start over and redo our failures, and creating beautiful new things in our lives. He works on us with love and patience. We can see that we are priceless to him because of all the effort it has taken to change us into the image of His Son. He will protect us diligently and He is determined to finish the good work He has begun.[15] One day, we will perfectly reflect the image of His Beloved Son, and He will present us to the One He dearly loves.[16] A priceless gift.

For I am confident of this very thing, that He who began a good work in you will perfect it until the day of Christ Jesus.

Philippians 1:6

Six

INVESTMENT

I remember sitting on the floor as a child, poring over colorful mail-order catalogs. They sported so many amazing toys that I did not have the funds to purchase: building sets, princess clothes, and best of all, toy horses. The toy horses I owned seemed to pale in comparison to the lovely flocked specimens in the catalog. Each time I perused the catalog, I longed for the time when I could buy one of my very own.

One day, I decided the time had come. What was the use in saving my money any longer? It was time to indulge. I would buy myself the black and white flocked horse with the feathery mane as soft as goose down.

A few weeks later, my horse arrived in the mail. By this time, the mesmerizing power of the mail-order catalog had diminished. I took the horse out of the box, wondering what had enticed me to spend so much of my meager savings.

As the years went by, the flocked horse sat in the toy room gathering dust. I learned that saving carefully was more important than satisfying my momentary cravings. For the next season of my life, I hoarded my money and refused to let it slip carelessly through my fingers.

Over the years, I learned of a third option for using my money: investing. As a child, I had considered investing my money by putting it in the bank. However, it seemed much more rewarding to see the bills and shiny golden dollar coins accumulate in my humble piggy.

It was only when I reached adulthood that investment finally made sense to me. I was excited to find an investor that would use my money wisely and pay high interest rates in return. At the same time, I felt a sense of disappointment as I signed the huge check that would deposit most of my money into their account.

Now I was poor.

Once again, I had emptied my piggy bank. Once again, my meager savings had disappeared from my grasp. But this time I had no flocked horse to show for it.

As I pondered my sudden poverty, I turned my thoughts to the future. Someday, after years of compounding interest, I would be glad I did not have money to spend right now. The money was not mine for now, yet at the same time it was mine for always. I was poor, yet at the same time I was rich.

In the Bible, Jesus talked about investing. The parable of the talents is a story of people who used their money to make more money. Jesus didn't tell this story to teach us how to manage our investment portfolios. Instead, He wanted us to see what we should do with our lives.

Jesus has given us a certain amount of time, love, and energy.[17] As Christians, we have a choice in how we will use the capital God has given us. We can use our time and energy on fulfilling our cravings and meeting our own desires. We can selfishly hoard it to give ourselves a sense of security. Or we can invest our energy and love in others.

Time invested in another person is lost for the present. The minutes used to send a note of hope and encouragement to a floundering friend can never be reused. Energy spent answering a child's endless questions can never be reclaimed. Love invested in another person may seem to be permanently lost when the other person rejects the love and friendship he has been offered.

But God promises that with persistence and patience, every investment made in His kingdom will pay high dividends. Whether now or in the life to come, the love we pour generously on others will be poured back into our laps—with interest.[18]

Seven

GO AHEAD AND FLY

"Carry me," begged little Ricky.

"You're getting heavy," I said, but I picked him up and continued walking down the street. I knew I wouldn't be able to carry him for much longer, so I treasured the chance to hold him close.

"Run," came the little voice. At first I hesitated, but he was insistent. "Please run."

I was young and strong. I could run with him in my arms. Why should I turn down such a kind and polite request? I jogged across the grass with him.

"Faster, please."

Although I was getting tired, I loved doing what made him happy. I loved the exhilarating exercise and the strength I was building as I barreled along with his little body securely tucked into my arms. This was becoming a routine, and I was getting better and faster each day.

Suddenly his voice surprised me. "Fly."

Fly! I gasped and laughed aloud. "Fly? What do you mean *fly?* I can carry you, I can run with you, I can run faster. But I can't fly! I just can't!"

"Fly please."

I still remember the feeling I had when I heard him asking me to fly. I couldn't believe my ears.

"What are you thinking? I'm strong, but I'm not that strong. Flying is impossible. I can't take off through the air, especially not with a heavy little boy in my arms."

God sometimes asks me to do something hard, like loving someone, forgiving someone, or obeying Him in a venture I've never attempted before. When I obey him, I get stronger. Then He asks me to do something harder, and I become even stronger spiritually. By the time I reach the third challenge, I'm thinking, "Wow, this is hard, but God is giving me more and more strength. It's exciting."

It's then that God asks me to do something so completely impossible that I sit back, shocked.

"What do you mean, 'Fly'?" I respond. "I can't fly. I'm strong, but not that strong. What You're asking is totally impossible, totally out of range."

There are times when even the spiritual strength I have built seems useless. I have to set out in total faith, believing that God will give the miraculous power to do what He has called me to do. God promises that those who trust in the Lord will not only walk without growing weary and run without fainting, but also mount up with wings like eagles.[19]

So if God has called you to do something that seems impossible, go ahead!

Yes, go ahead and fly!

Eight

FEARFUL, YET FOLLOWING

I knew Ricky would love the Museum of World Treasures. Situated in a large old building in the center of downtown, the museum promised glimpses of dinosaur bones and Egyptian relics. Ricky was currently fascinated by both subjects, and I imagined the awe and excitement he would feel when he saw real dinosaur bones and genuine Egyptian treasures. We planned to thoroughly enjoy the downstairs portion of the museum and then make our way to the children's room on the top level. This room was filled with small dinosaur toys, dragon puppets, knight costumes, a bouncy house, and almost everything else a four-year-old boy could wish for. I was confident that the admission cost would be money well spent.

As we entered the museum, my hopes were validated. Ricky was delighted by the small dinosaur statue in the entryway. The friendly T-Rex attracted him like a magnet.

Finally coaxing him away from the T-Rex, I led him through the gift shop. Once again he stopped and gaped at the shining swords on display.

"Let's go into the museum itself," I encouraged. The thrill of the entryway and gift shop was nothing compared to the excitement he was about to experience.

I led him past giant fossil reconstructions, shark replicas, and dinosaur models. He was mildly impressed, but motioned casually toward the entryway and said, "I think it was more fun to play with the little dinosaur out there."

Swiftly, I turned his attention to the Egyptian display.

"They have a real Egyptian mummy," I explained with excitement.

Terror replaced the joy in his face.

"Let's go back to the little dinosaur," he begged quickly.

"I paid way too much for this museum," I said, shocked. "We can't just leave after five minutes. Let's go to the children's room instead. You'll love it."

Confident that all was well, I led the way to the stairs. Half way up the flight of steps, I became aware of a voice drifting up at me from the ground level. My little friend was crying out with fear because of the open-back stairs.

"These stairs are scary! I'll fall! Let's go back and play with the little dinosaur!"

"Come on," I coaxed. "We can't go back. The stairs won't hurt you. Come on! You'll like the kids' room."

When we finally made it to the top of that flight of stairs, I opted to take the elevator the rest of the way to the top. Avoiding the remaining flights of stairs, we would ride the elevator straight to the children's room. But as I turned toward the elevator, he cried again in fear.

"Those soldiers are scary!" he sobbed as he glimpsed some life-sized historical soldier models representing different eras of military history. "Let's get out of here!"

"Just follow me. We have to go to the elevator if we want to get to the kids' room," I said with firmness in my voice.

When we finally reached the safety of the elevator, I gave a huge sigh of relief.

"We're almost there," I promised.

I stood quietly, allowing him to imagine the colorful children's room. The bouncy house, the castle, and the dinosaur toys would be well worth the trauma it had taken to reach this point.

But as the elevator came to a standstill, Ricky saw the doors open on a scene of tragic disappointment and betrayal.

There was no colorful kids' room in sight.

Before us stretched a vast banquet hall, silent and dark. It looked like ancient kings had been preparing for a feast when they had suddenly disappeared. Nothing was left behind except dark stillness. The only sound was the ancient ventilation system rattling into gear.

Ricky's mind struggled to grapple with his desperate disappointment. All the distress, fear, and torture he had endured seemed to be in vain. My promise was just a hollow lie of mockery.

"Come on, we're almost there!" My voice broke into his thoughts as I started out into the darkness.

"No!" he shouted in terror. "Let's get out of here. I won't follow you! I'm getting out of here."

As he huddled in the elevator, he must have wondered why he had believed me in the first place. If only he had stayed in the entryway with his little toy dinosaur. He had followed me through all those scary situations and now I was leaving him in the darkness.

No, I was not leaving him.

I was inviting him to follow.

In an instant, he made the choice. Despite his fear, despite his disappointment, and despite his disillusionment, he would follow.

And follow he did—right around the corner and into the bright children's room! Castles, dragon toys, a bouncy house, puzzles, dinosaurs, and armor kept him entranced the rest of the day. When the fading light of evening finally cast shadows across our long and happy play time, we retraced our steps through the banquet hall and down the elevator. To this day, my little friend remembers the fun he had in the Museum of World Treasures.

He does not dwell on the fear it took to get to that place. He just knows that my promises turned out to be true and he enjoyed them to the fullest.

In my life I have done the very same thing with God. He leads me through one scary experience after another, and just when I think the door will open on a beautiful reward, my hopes come crashing down around me. I feel He has forsaken me and tricked me in the worst way. But it's not true. His promises are real. He will not forsake me and He wants me to keep following through my fear and disappointment. He doesn't want me to give up and get out of here and quit on the life to which He has called me. It will be worth it in the end.

For I consider that the sufferings of this present time are not worth comparing with the glory that is going to be revealed to us.

Romans 8:18

Nine

LOUD LIGHTS

The distant moonlight reflected off the gentle waves lapping the seashore. The little turtle joined her brothers and sisters in their eager clamber to leave their sandy nest. As if drawn by an inner urgency, she turned herself toward the soft glow of the moon on the water. Hurrying toward the sea where she was created to live, she followed the instinct that would protect her from beach predators eager to eat young turtles.

Suddenly another light flashed on, brighter and nearer. The turtle siblings paused in their relentless journey toward the sea. Something was calling them to turn toward the brightest light available. Drawn by the powerful pull of two brightly lit street lamps, they turned their steps toward a nearby highway.

As they neared the busy thoroughfare, the turtles "were bombarded by lights and had no idea which way to turn."[20] One by one, six dozen little turtles flopped and scooted their way into the path of oncoming traffic. The little turtle pushed herself along to follow them.

Suddenly, a mix of blue and red lights flashed around the living turtles. "Police and bystanders" rushed to the rescue of the few that survived.[21] The littlest turtle felt a hand reaching down and picking her up.

The gentle hand carried her to the seashore where she had hatched and set her down inches from the water. Once again, she saw the dim moonlight shining from the rippling water. The pull inside her was strong. As she submerged herself and swam out to sea, she felt inner satisfaction. She was right where she was created to be.

In our lives, the voices that speak the loudest and demand the most attention are not always the truth. The direction that shines most brightly may not be the right path to follow. The pursuits that the majority rushes after may not truly give inner satisfaction.

Like moonlight, the light of God's word is steady, steadfast, and unchanging. Its voice does not clamor the loudest or demand most insistently. It quietly holds out its offer of life, hope, and fulfillment.

Popular opinion about the meaning of life leads people to scurry together toward the same dazzling light of earning, advancing, and succeeding. Many spend their entire lives chasing "achievement, comfort, [and] security."[22] Yet often they end up broken and empty.

When faced with the demands and expectations of society, remember that the closest, loudest, and most insistent voices may not be true. The Spirit of God dwelling within will guide you to follow the quiet glow of His word shining guidance into the darkest situations.[23] In the process, you will find satisfaction in the place you were created for.

And we have something more sure, the prophetic word, to which you will do well to pay attention as to a lamp shining in a dark place, until the day dawns and the morning star rises in your hearts.
2 Peter 1:19 ESV

My First Wheat Harvest

Ten

KANSAS GOLD

The engine of the combine harvester whirred steadily as we moved out into the field of waving wheat. Holding Ricky, I perched eagerly on the passenger's seat. The combine's teeth captured the golden wheat stalks, trimmed them at the base, and whisked them into the machine, leaving a wake of fresh yellow stubble. It was a beauty to behold.

Wheat harvest had been a yearly highlight for our family since I was two weeks old. I was pleased to pass on this special memory to Ricky, a fellow native Kansan. Together, we enjoyed the thrill of rustling golden wheat swelling in the Kansas breeze.

Wheat has not always been an emblem of our state. A hundred years before I was born, my ancestors immigrated to Kansas, bringing with them the finest seed wheat in the United States.[24] The "hand-selected grains of Turkey Red Wheat" formed the "basis of the abundant winter wheat crops that became an important part of the Kansas economy."[25]

The immigrants' children had spent countless hours choosing the most beautiful, firm, and healthy grains of wheat.[26] One by one the shriveled grains had been thrown out.[27] When they had filled their buckets with perfect grains, the immigrants left Crimea, Russia, and settled in Kansas.

The wheat was beautiful, high-quality, and valuable. It was the result of hours of diligent toil. Yet no one ever considered carefully preserving it in the barn for future generations. The wheat was quickly planted, producing a harvest that astounded the entire Kansas community.[28] Soon Kansas was called the Breadbasket of America.

Often we treat our lives, desires, and dreams as precious commodities which should be carefully preserved at all cost. On the other hand, Jesus sees our lives as seeds which must be lost in order to create a great harvest. Jesus explained, "I assure you: Unless a grain of wheat falls to the ground and dies, it remains by itself. But if it dies, it produces a large crop. The one who loves his life will lose it, and the one who hates his life in this world will keep it for eternal life."[29]

The Apostle Paul expressed the same willingness to lose his life in order to create a harvest. He said, "I count my life of no value to myself."[30] Paul was willing to make sacrifices like these so that others could be loved and saved, and begin growing in Christ. His life dropped out of sight like a tiny seed, covered by the dirt of messy problems, suffocated by the soil of trouble. Paul lost money, time and friends in order to show his love to Jesus and the others around him.

Sometimes Paul felt contagious joy about his sacrificial love for others. He told his friends, "Now I rejoice in my sufferings for you."[31] As his life was "poured out" for their spiritual well-being, he said, "I am glad and rejoice with all of you. In the same way you should be glad and rejoice with me."[32]

Other times, however, the daily sacrifice was mixed with heartache and near despair. Paul knew that his own selfless giving worked life in the Corinthians, yet the process was often difficult.[33] As he gave his life to the Corinthians, he became distressed and "hemmed in" with no way out.[34] Paul experienced the perplexity of being "at a loss," not knowing which way to turn.[35] At times, he faced the temptation to give up.[36]

Our lives are often like those grains of wheat: hand-selected, carefully prepared, and then buried beneath the dirt of disappointment and loss. During long days when the seed lies buried in the darkness and no life is visible, we must fight discouragement with the hope of a beautiful harvest.

Patient, O heart, though heavy be thy sorrows;
Be not cast down, disquieted in vain;
Yet shalt thou praise Him,
        when these darkened furrows,
Where now He plougheth,
        wave with golden grain.

        --Frederick L. Hosmer

Coryanthes Orchid

Eleven

THE ORCHID AND THE BEE

The male Euglossine bee circles the fragrant flower. The aroma of the Coryanthes orchid's sweet-smelling wax has captivated him with a power he cannot resist. Unknown to him, he has been created for a role that he alone can play. Only one species of bee can pollinate the orchid which has drawn his attention. Similarly, the orchid is essential and irreplaceable in the continuation of the bee species.[37] To fulfill his role, the male bee follows his powerful desire to reach the source of the fragrance. Little does he know the humiliating experience that awaits him.

The male Euglossine bee buzzes closer to the orchid's bucket, trying to find a way into the flower's hood.[38] Inside lies a fragrant substance that he needs to attract a mate. Below the hood hangs a bucket-shaped cup filled with clear, sticky liquid.

Many bright green Euglossine bees are swarming around the flower, and Mr. Glossy gets bumped and falls into the bucket. He tries his best to escape, but the bucket is lined with slippery hairs which make his exit impossible. His soaked wings are useless.[39] As he struggles and flounders in the bucket, he seems to have failed.

Finally, he finds a little step which leads to a tunnel.[40] It seems to be the only way out. He presses with all his might, hoping to come out on the other end. But again his hopes are dashed. There is no way out. The tunnel actually seems to be squeezing in around him on all sides. He is trapped.

Forty-five minutes later, the bee finally struggles out of the flower, wet and disheveled.[41] While trapped in the tunnel, a precious packet of pollen was glued onto his back. To complete the process, he will need to approach another orchid, and try once again.

The experience of struggling helplessly in the bucket of liquid "is so negative that the bee does not try it again for some time."[42] What if the bee refused to go near the flower again? What if he knew that he would slip again, and once again fall and almost drown? What if he knew he would struggle out, humiliated and wet? What if he resisted the feeling of being trapped in a dark tunnel, unable to make progress? What if he knew he would fly away from the flower a second time, feeling that he had accomplished nothing?

What if the bee tried once and said, "Never again! I am a failure at this."

The bee would have no idea that precious pollen had been deposited on his back. The bucket, the slippery slope, and the constricting tunnel were all parts of one grand design. Because of his humiliating experience, the bee now carried the key to the future continuation of the orchid species.

The despairing bee would not know that if he tried one more time he would produce life. As he would fall again, struggle again, and be trapped again, the precious pollen would slip off his back into the heart of the flower, allowing the flower to produce seeds and more orchid plants.

He would fly away feeling like he had failed again. Although he had not reached the perfume his heart desired, he had created life in the heart of another.

In the Bible, the Apostle Paul tried again and again to preach the gospel. He shared God's word in Thessalonica and Corinth but escaped each city humiliated, disgraced, and trapped in persecution. Paul felt overwhelmed and fearful.[43]

Although Paul departed from each city with nothing but struggles and fear in his own heart, he left behind life in the hearts of others! He had delivered the "pollen" of truth that later grew into a church filled with hope, love, and faith.[44]

Have you tried again and again on a relationship, endeavor, or ministry for the Lord? Have you reaped nothing but apparent failure? If God created you with this calling and desire, you are uniquely suited for the task He has assigned. God may be accomplishing things through you that you simply cannot see. Although you may not have reached the "perfume" that you so desired, your faithfulness may have brought life to someone else—life that you cannot yet see.

Finally, after many attempts, the Euglossine bee reaches the treasure chests of fragrant sweetness hidden deep within the flower. Other bees around him reached their goal long ago. Finding the aromatic wax on the first attempt, they have long since moved on. They know the carefree joy of victory, but they have never experienced the long-lasting reward of crawling out defeated... and leaving life behind.

The credit belongs to the man who is actually in the arena, whose face is marred by dust and sweat and blood;

who strives valiantly; who errs, who comes short again and again, because there is no effort without error and shortcoming;

but who does actually strive to do the deeds;

who knows great enthusiasms, the great devotions; who spends himself in a worthy cause;

who at the best knows in the end the triumph of high achievement, and who at the worst, if he fails, at least fails while daring greatly, so that his place shall never be with those cold and timid souls who neither know victory nor defeat.

--Theodore Roosevelt

Twelve

CREATED FOR SERVICE

I remember the paralyzing panic I felt when Ricky, a toddler at the time, fell down the stairs and hurt his head. I held him on my lap, unable to think clearly about what should be done. Eventually I gathered my thoughts and found the information I needed to help him. But even more quickly, his own body had mobilized to bring healing to his injury.

God has created the human body in a marvelous way. Despite the fog of pain and the clamor of fear, the body responds instantly to come to the rescue of a wounded member. Each part knows its job and jumps in to help the hurting part as soon as it possibly can. With guidance from the brain's knowledge of first aid, the parts of our body work together as an excellent team.

Each part of the body was made to serve a specific fellow body part, while other parts of the body are clearly *not* the best ones to help. Think about the eye and the hand. Usually the eye washes itself with tears and blinking. But if something too big and too overwhelming gets stuck in the eye, it needs help. It doesn't need help from the foot, the lymph, or even the diaphragm. It needs help from the hand, and quickly. While one eye looks in the mirror to help determine what is needed, the hand rubs the wounded eye and gently removes the foreign particle. God gives this example in 1 Corinthians 12:21: "So the eye cannot say to the hand, 'I don't need you.'"

Or how about the food which goes down the wrong pipe? At this point the lymph, the foot, and the elbow are helpless. The only part which can help the body is the diaphragm. Sending a strong puff of air to dislodge the food, the diaphragm must do its job as quickly as it can before the person stops breathing and dies.

Believers who trust in Christ for salvation are bound together in one body by one Spirit as members of each other. You have a job to do in the body of Christ.[45] You have other brothers and sisters in Christ depending on you, and you on them. When another believer whom you know and love is struggling, should you just stand by watching them suffer? God instructs, "Brothers, if someone is caught in any wrong-doing, you who are spiritual should restore such a person with a gentle spirit, watching out for yourselves so you also won't be tempted. Carry one another's burdens; in this way you will fulfill the law of Christ."[46] Be at their side, assuring them you will be there to help in any way you can.

At other times, you may have a less prominent role in restoring the other person. Consider how well you know the person and their circumstances. If you jump into their situation and into their life without knowing their heart, their motives, and the details of their situation, you may hurt them further. If you jump to conclusions and attempt to correct a person whom you do not know well and who does not have a relationship with you, you may be just as ineffective as a foot trying to remove a splinter from the eye.[47]

You are made for a purpose within the body of Christ. There are parts of the body that are depending on you. Don't let them down. At the same time, be careful not to judge someone before you know their situation. Ask God to give you gentleness, wisdom, and love so you can do your part in His body and in His work in the world.

But now God has placed each one of the parts in one body just as He wanted.

1 Corinthians 12:18

Thirteen

LEANING ON THE PROMISES

It was fun riding bike when he was four. He soared and bumped across the grass propelled by nothing but his own two feet.

As time went on, Ricky received a new bike with training wheels. It was much easier this way, and he loved spending his afternoons rolling down the sidewalk at top speed.

Ricky used his bike to the max, until the training wheels were bent and the bike leaned to one side as it careened down the sidewalk. Still, he kept riding. He loved his bicycle!

Finally I decided it was time for him to graduate back to two wheels. I brought out the big bike and off we went.

Crash! He was on the ground before he had gone three feet. Dusting himself off and trying again, he was once again disappointed by promptly falling to the ground.

After spending months on a tilted bike, Ricky had become accustomed to leaning to one side while riding. Now that the bike was straight, he crashed over when he started his habitual leaning.

I told him that it was normal to fall while learning, but he became very fearful. Every attempt ended in failure, and he was soon hysterical and vowed never to ride bike again.

Finally I made a compromise.

Despite the fact that all children should be allowed the chance to fall while learning, I made him a radical promise: "I will never let you fall. I will never let go of you. I will hold you up. Even if you've fallen before, I will not let you fall now."

Ricky trembled because he wouldn't believe me. He didn't believe that after falling so many times, he wouldn't fall this time. He didn't believe that I would keep my word if I had let him get hurt in the past. He refused to ride the bike because he flatly disbelieved my promises.

I was sad, but I continued holding out the promise: I will not fail you.

Almost a year later, he finally agreed to get back on a bicycle. It seemed safe to climb on the back of a tandem bicycle with Dad firmly holding up the front of the bike. Dad would direct the bike, hold it up, and be with him the whole way. All Ricky had to do was hold tight and keep his feet in the pedals.

As Dad's promise to hold him up became reality every time, Ricky decided to try his own bike again. Because of his fears, I promised I would hold him up even on his own little bike. Gradually he gained strength, balance, and trust.

Every time Ricky rode his bike, I held the bike up and steered. This continued until one day, he told me he was ready to do it by himself. He took his falls with manly determination until one day, he was soaring down the sidewalk with confidence.

As I watched him go through this agonizing process, I prayed, "Lord, please make me willing to put my full weight on Your promises."

Despite my fear, I can approach a situation in which I have fallen in the past. I can trust His extravagant promises to be with me,[48] to never leave me,[49] and to constantly hold onto me.[50] He promises that He is able to keep me exempt from falling and bring me with great joy into His kingdom.[51]

I can get on that "bike" and go on with Christ, resting on His promises. All I need to do is hold onto His grace and keep my feet in the pedals of obedience.[52]

I can trust extravagantly if I'm leaning on Him and doing His will. He will not fail.

Trust in the Lord with all your heart, and do not lean on your own understanding. In all your ways acknowledge him, and he will make straight your paths.

Proverbs 3:5-6 ESV

Protected Palms

Fourteen

POLISHED ARROW

The remains of a beautiful acacia tree littered the African soil. Clusters of yellow pom-pom flowers were strewn across the ground, torn from the trees that gave them life and beauty. Shattered leaves and shreds of bark lay scattered beneath bare branches.

Missionary Helen Roseveare thoughtfully surveyed the ruin.[53] Although the destruction of these trees had been intentional and deliberate, it was not senseless. Helen knew that branch by branch, the tree was being employed for a greater purpose.

Bright yellow weaver birds had invaded the town and plundered the palm nuts growing among the fringes of palm trees in the village. The nuts were valued for the palm oil they produced for the villagers. Eager to save the palm nuts, Helen had offered the neighborhood children a prize for each weaver bird they killed.

Immediately branches began to disappear indiscriminately from nearby trees. After cutting the twigs, children fashioned them into arrows to shoot at the offending birds. Quickly, Helen placed the citrus trees off-limits, but allowed the children to use acacia branches to make arrows. The beautiful flowers and lovely foliage of the acacia would have to be sacrificed to save the palms.

The children worked diligently and ruthlessly to create a weapon that would effectively fulfill their purpose. They chose straight twigs that would make strong arrows, then stripped off the bright yellow flowers that the tree had needed for reproduction and beauty. Removing the leaves that were vital to the tree's nourishment, they cut away the thorns that protected the branch and the bark that kept out disease and harm.

What remained of the twig was bare and helpless. Everything that had made it beautiful and useful had been taken away. If it were thrown aside now, it would be utterly without value. Empty and bare, it would quickly die.

The diligent young arrow-maker did not even consider carelessly throwing his branch aside. Focused on the reward he would receive for destroying the enemies of the oil supply, he quickly finished the arrow he had begun. In the hands of the expert craftsman, the branch was smoothed, carved, and transformed into something new: an arrow to protect the precious palm nuts.

The Lord Jesus Christ is an expert craftsman, shaping our lives for His loving purposes. As He skillfully works in our stories and situations, His hands may at times seem ruthless. We tremble as He removes things that we needed for our beauty, nourishment, and success. We lose things we thought were vital to our identity, and to our continuation and preservation and replication. Things that promised us security and protection sometimes vanish as He works in our lives. Following Jesus sometimes means losing everything we have.[54]

When we come to Him, trusting Him to create us into something useful for His glory, God often removes things that we think we need.[55]

He takes away things that will hinder us from accomplishing His purpose. He removes sins and takes away our self-protection. In the process, we feel useless for any other purpose. If He would set us aside now, we would be totally without options. But in the hands of the master carver we are suited perfectly for the purpose for which He created us.[56]

As an arrow, I can fly farther and serve him better than I ever could as a flowery, showy branch. I can protect other people with my prayers so they can serve Him and bring glory to Him. Isaiah 49 tells me that without Him, I feel useless.[57] But with His help, I can go to other lands as His ambassador.[58] I can fly free and multiply in ways I never dreamed possible.[59] Was the loss worth it? Yes. Beyond a doubt.

The Lord called me before I was born. He named me while I was in my mother's womb… He made me like a sharpened arrow; He hid me in His quiver. But I myself said: I have labored in vain, I have spent my strength for nothing and futility; yet my vindication is with the LORD, and my reward is with my God.

Isaiah 49:1-2, 4

Fifteen

TEAM PERSPECTIVE

"Which one is clearer: this... or this?" The eye doctor sat back, waiting for my answer. I held a black spoon over one eye as he flipped his lenses over the open eye.

Finally he asked me to take the black spoon away. I gasped at the beautiful, perfect image I saw.

"The eyes are a great team, aren't they?" he asked. "The eyes can see so much better together than either one of them can by itself."

With only one eye open, it is difficult to tell if something is flat or deep, close or far away. One eye can misjudge the depth of something. A person using only one eye can stumble when walking over an uneven surface because of a lack of depth perception. But two eyes working together give perspective, clarity, and beauty.

God has created believers to work together as a body, as a team. One person by himself can easily lose perception. By myself I can misjudge the depth, importance, or relative significance of a certain event or situation. My emotions can blow something out of proportion and make it more important than it really is. I can misjudge distances and fail to see the closeness of God or the sureness of His reward in heaven.

One believer by himself easily falls captive to false philosophy and deception. It is much easier to stumble when you are on your own.

That is why God encourages people to bind together in a loving body. Other Christians add depth, perspective, and truth to a believer's life. God commands His followers to encourage each other so that they are not hardened by sin.[60] Frequently meeting with other Christians helps prevent willful disobedience.[61] A strong, encouraging bond with God's children helps believers avoid falling into deception.[62]

The eyes are a beautiful team. Yes, they can function independently, but most of the time they don't think twice about moving together, looking together, opening and shutting together, and focusing together.

When the eyes work together in perfect harmony, they are lovely and attractive. When we as believers feel, think, and love as one,[63] we create an irresistible beauty that reflects the face of Christ to the world.[64]

Sixteen

SAFETY IN THE DEEP

One of the most beautiful sights of the sea is a stream of silvery schooling fish. They swim as a unit made up of hundreds of parallel flashes of light. Moving together around obstacles, they ebb and flow like a stream of liquid silver. When approached by a large predatory fish, the group bursts open like a firework, only to rejoin in ever-faithful unity and symmetry.

The schooling instinct of anchovies and sardines is a method of protection and safety. As the fish shimmer in the sunlight, flowing together in the same direction, it is difficult for predators to distinguish where one silvery body ends and another begins. There is safety in numbers.

The fish follow three simple rules: stay close to each other, go the "same direction," and "avoid collisions."[65] In this way they form themselves into a beautiful work of art, as if "choreographed" to a grand unheard symphony.[66]

When the school moves together in the deep recesses of the sea, it is relatively safe. However, some large predatory fish have discovered a method to conquer members of the school. By herding the group toward the surface, enemies such as sailfish corner the small fish against the impenetrable surface of the water.[67] "Panic results, [and] each individual in the school goes into a self-preservation mode by abandoning the collective good of the school and diving right in towards the relative safety of the center of the pack."[68]

The result is a sphere called a bait ball which has none of the safety functions of a school. Sailfish and other enemies dart into the middle of this easy target, spearing, shredding, and shattering the individual fish. In the wild, the entire bait ball often meets a grisly end. However, some of the fish may escape to the deep water where they are safe. Fish may hide under the body of a scuba diver, since predators are wary of approaching a human. Once again, the fish are safe.

The body of Christ is a beautiful unity formed out of diversity. Like schooling fish which "can literally feel the other fish at a distance,"[69] Christ has given his people the privilege of sharing the same Holy Spirit which allows them to empathize with each other in powerful ways.[70] This allows them to cooperate in beautiful unity and harmony.

A school of fish "moves through the water as if directed by a collective brain."[71] In a similar way, the body of Christ functions as a whole and is directed by an unseen Head. He controls its movement and harmonizes its individual parts in one beautiful unity.[72]

At the same time, Satan and his evil followers are always seeking to destroy the beauty, harmony, and safety found in His body.[73] If the enemy can use his skill to herd the flock away from deep commitment to Christ, he can corner them near the surface and distract them with superficial concerns.[74] If the enemy can wound and terrify the body of Christ, individuals may shift their focus to self-preservation and become far more vulnerable to destruction.

What is the secret to a beautiful unity that can survive the constant attacks of the evil one? The answer is found in hiding in Christ, in "holding fast to the Head, from whom all the body, nourished and knit together by joints and ligaments, grows with the increase that is from God."[75] The answer is diving together into deep consecration, deep love, deep commitment, and deep humility. In the deep, there is safety.

Go deep. Avoid collision. Stay close.

Seventeen

CHRYSALIS

I once was a creature with stripes strong and bold,

Of deepest rich black and of loveliest gold.

I moved about freely, vivacious and strong,

Until one bright day I felt change coming on.

My gold and black skin

  was beginning to burst.

I felt that this life change

  could not be reversed.

Inside my chrysalis, I went through a change.

Each part of my life would be now rearranged.

I trembled as I realized the life-changing cost.

All I had once known was apparently lost.

My brain and my body were turning to mush,

And the outcome of this was not easily rushed.

Now helpless and muted, I could not respond.

I was tied to a twig with a strong, silky bond.

I waited with purpose for many a day

As God's plan unfolded in His perfect way.

Now I can see that this time had a reason,

Although it was hard, it was only a season.

I now am a creature with marks strong and bold,

Of deepest rich black and of loveliest gold.

I move about freely, gentle and wise,

For only through waiting are born butterflies.

Those who wait upon the Lord will gain new strength; They will mount up with wings…

Isaiah 40:31

NOTES

How This Book Came to Be
[1] Matthew 18:5

Chapter 1
[2] Romans 8:32
[3] Romans 1:21-32
[4] To learn more about coming to the Lord Jesus Christ for salvation, please see http://www.lifein6words.com/#sthash.CWsVXhf8.dpbs
[5] Ephesians 2:8-9
[6] John 15:14

Chapter 2
[7] YouTube, "Natural Horse Training Approaching Unbroken Horse," http://www.youtube.com/watch?v=3uPQ8XFPMB0, Accessed September 7, 2013

[8] Linda Aronson, "Fear in Horses," *Pet Place*, www.petplace.com/horses/fear-in-horses/page1.aspx, Accessed October 14, 2013
[9] Ibid.

Chapter 3
[10] Exodus 6:1 ESV
[11] Numbers 11:23

Chapter 4
[12] Strong's Concordance, Bible Hub, http://biblesuite.com/greek/1476.htm. Accessed September 11, 2013.
[13] 1 Corinthians 15:58 NASB

Chapter 5
[14] Hebrews 13:21, Romans 8:29
[15] Philippians 1:6
[16] Mark 1:11, 2 Corinthians 4:14

Chapter 6
[17] Sam Doherty, *Smooth Sailing in Relationships and Leadership,* (Lisburne, UK: Child Evangelism Fellowship, 1999), 115
[18] Luke 6:38

Chapter 7
[19] Isaiah 40:31

Chapter 9
[20] *Orlando Sentinel,* "Turtles Crushed on Road," http://articles.orlandosentinel.com/1995-07-25/news/9507250165_1_sea-turtles-volusia-county-street-lights, Accessed October 18, 2013

[21] Ibid.

[22] "The Sermon on the Mount," part 3, Lesson 7 Series III (San Antonio: Bible Study Fellowship, 2013) 5

[23] 2 Peter 1:19

Chapter 10

[24] Krahn, Cornelius. (1959). Wheat. *Global Anabaptist Mennonite Encyclopedia Online.* http://gameo.org/index.php?title=Wheat&oldid=859 89, Accessed November 8, 2013.

[25] Mansur G. Abdullah, ed. Et. Al., *Encyclopaedia Brittanica,* http://www.britannica.com/EBchecked/topic/6099 43/Turkey-Red-wheat, Accessed November 8, 2013

[26] Bliss Isely, *Early Days in Kansas,* (Wichita: Eagle Printing and Lithograph Company, 1967), 151

[27] Ibid.

[28] Ibid.

[29] John 12:24-25

[30] Acts 20:24

[31] Colossians 1:24

[32] Philippians 2:17-18, see also Colossians 1:24

[33] 2 Corinthians 4:12

[34] Strong's Concordance, *Bible Hub,* http://biblesuite.com/greek/2346.htm, Accessed October 25, 2013, see 2 Corinthians 4:8

[35] Strong's Concordance, *Bible Hub,* http://biblesuite.com/greek/639.htm, Accessed October 25, 2013

[36] 2 Corinthians 4:16

Chapter 11

[37] Dr. Günter Gerlach, "The Species Coryanthes," Botanischer Garten München-Nymphenburg,

http://www.botmuc.de/en/about/guenter_gerlach/genus_coryanthes.html, Accessed November 1, 2013
[38] Yoder, Pablo, *The Works of His Fingers,* (Harrisonburg: Christian Light Publications, 2009) 74
[39] Dr. Günter Gerlach, "The Species Coryanthes" Botanischer
[40] Yoder, Pablo, *The Works of His Fingers,* 74
[41] Dr. Günter Gerlach, "The Species Coryanthes"
[42] Ibid.
[43] 2 Corinthians 7:6
[44] 1 Thessalonians 1:3

Chapter 12
[45] Ephesians 4:16
[46] Galatians 6:1-2
[47] Luke 6:41-42

Chapter 13
[48] Joshua 1:9
[49] Hebrews 13:5
[50] John 10:28-29
[51] Jude 1:24
[52] Hebrews 12:28

Chapter 14
[53] Helen Roseveare, *Living Sacrifice* (Scotland: Christian Focus Publishers, 2007), 23-27
[54] Matthew 19:29
[55] Hebrews 12:1-2
[56] Ephesians 2:10, Philippians 1:6
[57] Isaiah 49:4
[58] Isaiah 49:1-3, 5-6
[59] Isaiah 49:18-23

Chapter 15

[60] Hebrews 3:13
[61] Hebrews 10:24-26
[62] Colossians 2:2-8, Ephesians 4:11-16
[63] Philippians 2:1-3
[64] 2 Corinthians 4:6, John 17:23

Chapter 16

[65] "Baitball," *Wikipedia,*
http://en.wikipedia.org/wiki/Baitball, Accessed
January 31, 2013
[66] Ibid.
[67] Ibid.
[68] Mark H. "Marine Life Series: Bait Balls"
http://www.dailykos.com/story/2008/12/04/6694
62/-Marine-Life-Series-Bait-Balls, Accessed February
1, 2013
[69] Doug Perrine, Guy Harvey Magazine, "Mysteries of
the Bait Ball,"
http://guyharveymagazine.com/topics/
aquaculture/mysteries-bait-ball, Accessed September
7, 2013
[70] Philippians 2:1-3, 1 Corinthians 12:13
[71] Mark H. "Marine Life Series: Bait Balls," Accessed
February 1, 2013
[72] 1 Corinthians 12:11, 24-25, Colossians 2:19
[73] Acts 20:29
[74] Colossians 2:16-23
[75] Colossians 2:19 NKJV

Made in the USA
Charleston, SC
08 March 2014